THE GIANT
PANDA

Discovering China

THE GIANT PANDA

FANG MIN

Better Link Press

Copyright © 2011 Shanghai Press and Publishing Development Company

This book is edited and designed by the Editorial Committee of *Cultural China* series

Managing Directors: Wang Youbu, Xu Naiqing
Editorial Director: Wu Ying
Editor: Zhang Yicong

Text by Fang Min
Photographs by Fang Min, Hou Xiaojun, Zhang Guiquan, Liu Weixin and Quanjing
Translation by Ben Daggers

Interior and Cover Design: Wang Wei
Cover Image: Getty Images

ISBN: 978-1-60220-130-9

Address any comments about *Discovering China: The Giant Panda* to:

Better Link Press
99 Park Ave
New York, NY 10016
USA

or

Shanghai Press and Publishing Development Company
F 7 Donghu Road, Shanghai, China (200031)
Email: comments_betterlinkpress@hotmail.com

Printed in China by Shenzhen Donnelley Printing Co. , Ltd.

1 3 5 7 9 10 8 6 4 2

CONTENTS

A Giant Panda in the forest (provided by Quanjing)

Prologue

My Name Is Baiyun

My name is Baiyun (literally "White Cloud") and I was born in 1991 among the verdant mountains and clear waters of the Wolong Giant Panda Center. It was there, under the loving, watchful eye of the Wolong folk, that I spent my childhood. In 1996 I left my homeland for the United States of America, and it was here that Shishi and I fell for one another. On August 21st 1999, my first child was born, a beautiful girl who was given the name Huamei. In 2003, Shishi returned to his native China, and my life with an older man was over. Later that year, Gaogao arrived in the U.S., and suddenly there was a new man in my life. Gaogao, whose age was similar to mine, was a strapping, dashing fellow who hailed from the wilderness of the Fengtong Valley Nature Reserve in the Qionglai Mountains. As he was from the same neck of the woods as my father, the two of us hit it off straight away, and before long a full-blown romance had blossomed. On August 19th 2003 my son Meisheng was born, and on August 2nd 2005 he was *joined by his sister Sulin. On August 3rd 2007 I was blessed with yet another daughter, Zhenzhen, and in 2009, at the ripe old age of eighteen, I gave birth to Yunzi.*

Life away from home has flown by, and in the blink of an eye the flower of youth has given way to old age. In 2004, my oldest daughter Huamei had a child of her own, and I am now a grandmother.

Though I want for nothing here, surrounded by family and cared for and doted on by the American people, thoughts of my birthplace, my clan, my siblings and my homeland do still creep in during the long, quiet nights. Years pass, yet night after night, all of these thoughts flash before my eyes, and linger in my dreams.

Chapter One

Our Three Million-year March from the Past to Today

Bai Yun: Nowadays, many people say that we are an endangered species, a powerless group on the brink of extinction. Little do they know that ever since emerging as a species, we pandas have continued to flourish in the face of unimaginable hardship, marching on undeterred no matter what life throws at us...

We have no way of seeing into the past of ancient species, and can only imagine what life was like for them based on the findings of palaeontologists.

In the past hundred years, palaeontologists in Asia, and particularly in China, have uncovered nearly one hundred Giant Panda fossil sites. These fossils reveal the entire evolutionary process of the panda, from its speciation into the early panda and evolution into the Pygmy Giant Panda and *A.M.baconi*, right through to its modern day incarnation.

In 1989, in the lignite beds of Lufeng, Yunnan Province, a series of partial dental fossils belonging to early pandas were found, which were given the name *A.lufengensis*. In 1991, fossils containing the upper jaw and part of the cheekbone were discovered in Yunnan's Yuanmou County, which were named Yuanmo Panda (*A.yuanmouensis*). This concluded the search for the earliest direct ancestor of the Giant Panda which had lasted for over a century. They lived approximately eight or nine million years ago during the middle Miocene Epoch, and dwelt in the marshlands. Though somewhat smaller in size than the Lesser Giant Panda of the early Pleistocene Epoch, their teeth were similar in shape, establishing their kinship with the Giant Panda.

Since then, in the lignite beds of France and Hungary which

The Zhoukoudian in Beijing, the most northerly point reached by Giant Pandas in their heyday

date back to the late Miocene Epoch some six million years ago, examples of early Giant Panda have been discovered, whose teeth bear even closer similarity to Giant Panda species, which have been named *A.goali*. Regrettably, they have no direct descendents, and represent a dead-end in the taxonomy of the Giant Panda.

In 1943, the Chinese Palaeontologist Pei Wenzhong unearthed four Giant Panda jawbones and seventy-two teeth at Guangxi Province's Juyuan Cave, which date back 1.8 million years to the early Pleistocene Epoch, providing a further branch from the early panda. They were somewhat larger in size than the early panda, and had already fully evolved into a species of their own—the Pygmy Giant Panda (*A.microta*).

In later years, Pygmy Giant Panda fossils were excavated in Guangdong Province's Gouwei Embankment, as well as Sichuan Province's Damiaolonggu slope, and Shaanxi Province's Jinshui Estuary. This shows that their territory extended northwards from the Yunnan-Guizhou Plateau, right through to the southern face of the Qinling Mountains, which today separate the Chinese mainland into north and south. During this period, there were approximately thirty animal species which lived alongside the Pygmy Giant Panda, which have collectively been dubbed "Gigantopithecus." Of these, the vast majority clearly share many traits with the fauna found in the Pacific region, including Asian tropical and subtropical animals such as primates and elephants, grass and dryland animals including Yunnan horses and hyaena, forest and plain-dwelling animals such as cheetahs, and marsh-dwellers including tapir and rhinoceros.

It is clear that *A.microta* lived in tropical or subtropical forests which enjoyed heavy rainfall, which were dotted with grasslands, marshes and rivers. As the region expanded and the habitat became richer, the Giant Panda expanded in numbers and thrived as a species.

During the middle Pleistocene Epoch six or seven hundred thousand years ago, *A.microta*'s time in the spotlight began drawing to a close. This was brought about in large part by *A.M.baconi*, whose skull was similar in structure to *A.microta*, yet larger than both *A.microta*, and even the modern Giant Panda.

From the early to late Pleistocene Epoch, a period which spanned some seven hundred thousand years, *A.M.baconi* expanded in both numbers and territory, extending into the Yellow, Yangtze, and Zhujiang River regions. They spread west to Myanmar and Thailand, south to Vietnam and China's Taiwan, and north to Pinglu and Zhoukoudian, both of which lie in the

The ancient Katsura Tree, which along with Giant Pandas represents one of natures great survivors

Bashania fargesii is a favourite among Qinling Giant Pandas

northern half of China, in what was an unprecedented purple patch in the history of the Giant Panda.

Eighteen thousand years ago during the late Pleistocene Epoch, after the Fourth Ice Age had wrought its devastation, the bitter weather, frozen land and lack of food drove the Giant Panda, as well as many other species, to the brink of collapse. Large species such as the Stegodont (elephant), tapir, rhinoceros and Gigantopithecus all began to die out, and *A.M.baconi* too began the slow march to extinction. It was during these perilous times that the Giant Panda

The "false" thumb of the Giant Panda

Giant Pandas are classified as carnivores, yet through their long and protracted evolution have come to subsist primarily on bamboo. Their front paws have evolved accordingly. In terms of anatomy, the "thumb" of the panda is strictly speaking not a thumb at all, but is a radial sesamoid bone formed from the wrist. The radial sesamoid supports the pad above it, while the other five fingers form another pad. Between these two pads lies a shallow channel, which they use to grip the bamboo. The renowned American natural historian Stephen Jay Gould has classed the panda's "thumb" as "an exquisite structure."

began to change its carnivorous eating habits, most notably by adopting bamboo as its main source of food, ensuring the continued survival of the species.

Disaster was not completely averted, however. As man extended his reach south of the Qinling Mountains, the valleys and mountains around the Yangtze and Zhujiang Rivers were rapidly reclaimed. Giant Panda territory was driven back towards the edge of the Qinghai-Tibet Plateau, as the pandas seized upon what limited space they could find in remote mountainous regions such as Qionglai, Minshan, Liangshan and Xiangling, where man had not yet staked his claim. In the face of diminished territory, depleted numbers, and a frame some eleven or twelve percent smaller than *A.M.baconi*, the stubborn will to survive of these pandas led to their gradual evolution into the Giant Panda as we know it today (*A.melanoleuca*).

The passing of time can yield great change. And so it was that this ancient species came into existence. It endured weakness to become strong; struggled at the hands of its own prosperity; and finally, in the depths of this struggle, found a way to survive.

Chapter Two

We Are Named, and the World's Eyes Fall on Us

Baiyun: In order to escape man's fervent expansion, our forefathers were pushed back ever further, leaving the fertile soil, plains, and hills behind in favour of Western China's lofty mountains, deep canyons, and ancient forests. There, they could live in peace, eating bamboo and drinking spring water free from human meddling. Yet the arrival of a French priest was to change all that...

Dengchi Valley Catholic Church from afar

In Muping Town's Dengchi Valley, on the western edge of Sichuan Province, there is a Catholic church which has stood since 1839. From afar, its pointed, grey-tiled roof resembles that of a typical Chinese courtyard domecile, yet upon closer inspection, its vast sense of solemnity, lotus petal-like arched ceilings and stained glass windows betray its strong Western roots. In 1867, a Frenchman named Jean Pierre Armand David arrived, becoming the church's fourth priest. 130 years later, as we looked through Father David's diary, we discovered that during his spell as Dengchi Valley Church priest, David de-

View from inside the Dengchi Valley Church

voted considerable time and energy to seeking out the strange and wonderful flora and fauna of the mountains. Thus, he was able to lift the veil of mystery which had previously surrounded this most reclusive of species.

Père Armand David in Chinese dress

46-year-old Father David wearing Qing-dynasty dress

David writes:

March 11th, 1869

Upon returning from an excursion we are invited to rest at the home of a certain Li, the principal landowner in the valley, who serves us tea and sweets. At this pagan's I see a fine skin of the famous white and black bear {Ailuropoda melanoleucus}, which appears to be fairly large. It is a remarkable species and I am delighted when I hear my hunters say that I shall certainly obtain the animal within a short time. They tell me they will go out tomorrow to kill this animal, which will provide an interesting novelty for science.

The backyard of the Dengchi Valley Church

21

The controversy in classification

In 1869, Father David described the panda specimen as a "white and black bear" (*Urus melanoleucus David*). That same year the Muséum national d'Histoire chief Milne Edwards claimed the specimen was similar to bears in appearance alone, and that structurally it was closer to little pandas and racoons, classing it a black and white panda (*A.melanoleuca*). Since the name panda already denoted the small pandas discovered in 1825, the larger variety was given the name Giant Panda. As to whether the Giant Panda should be classified with the bears or racoons, consensus is still divided some 130 years after the debate started. Prior to the 1980s opinion was divided into three schools: some classed it with the bears, some with racoons, and others in a class of its own. Gradually, one group was dismissed, and today opinion is divided between the bear and giant panda factions.

March 23rd, 1869

My Christian hunters return today after a ten day absences. They bring me a young white bear, which they took alive but unfortunately killed so it could be carried more easily. The young white bear, which they sold to me very dearly, is all white except for the legs, ears, and around the eyes, which are deep black. The colors are the same as those I saw in the skin of an adult bear the other day at the home of Li, the hunter. This must be a new species of Ursus {Ailuropoda}, very remarkable not only because of its color, but also for its paws, which are hairy underneath, and for other characteristics.

April 1st, 1869

They bring me a white bear {Ailuropoda melanoleucus} which they tell me is fully adult. Its colors are exactly like those of the young one I have, only the darker parts are less black and the white more soiled. The animal's head is very big, and the snout round and short instead of being pointed as it is in the Pekin bear.

April 7th, 1869

They bring me another live panda. This animal does not look fierce, and behaves like a little bear. Its paws and head exactly resemble those of my white bear. Its stomach is full of leaves.

The "white bear" which the hunters caught for Father David was the specimen taken back to Paris, whereupon Milne Edwards, head of Paris' Muséum national d'Histoire, confirmed Father David's finding, naming it the Giant Panda.

The discovery of this new species caused a stir in the Western world, and explorers from all quarters at once fell into action. The most famous case is that of former United States President Roosevelt's two sons, Theodore and Kermit Roosevelt, who twice came to China to hunt Giant Panda in the Qionglai Mountains.

In the Spring of 1926, two foreigners arrived in Muping Town's Shanggan Valley. The brothers, both growing a beard and a moustache, stayed with their host Wang Haitang in his home, along with their interpreter and two cooks. They spent all day in the mountain forests, and before they knew it several days had passed. For fear of becoming lost, the brothers recruited locals who could guide them and carry their belongings. Each day they would reward them with a one *yuan* note,

The two Roosevelt brothers, Theodore (left) and Kermit (right) who went hunting for Giant Pandas

or occasionally two strings of copper coins.

The light breeze, fine clouds and perfect visibility meant for a perfect day's hunting, and it afforded them an encounter with a Giant Panda. The elder brother saw it first and winked at his younger brother. They took aim and fired simultaneously, hitting the panda on its leg. The group descended upon the downed creature, hurriedly tied it up before taking it back to their host's home. The following day, the injured panda was placed in a cage, and was originally bound for America, though unfortunately died on the way.

In Spring 1928, these two foreigners came to visit again, yet again as Wang Haitang's guests, expressing their desire to hunt unicorns in Wutan Snow Mountains.

Deep in the Wutan Snow Mountains is a lake, which according to legend was home to a unicorn, who would often harm hunters in the area. In Wang Haitang's eyes, killing this beast was a good thing, and so dispatched tens of locals to help.

The men trekked on horseback for three days before reaching the lake. There was not a sound on the limpid, still lake, though a group of golden monkeys could be heard bounding through the nearby fir trees. The sound of gunshots soon filled the air, and when silence was restored, fourteen golden monkeys had been killed, which were then carried down the mountain and kept as specimens.

The Giant Panda's name

The name "Giant Panda" appeared in print for the first time in a French zoological magazine in 1870. Descriptions of animals whose apperance and habits are identical to Giant Pandas can be found in many old Chinese writings, however. Various sources have given more than twenty names to the creature, including *pixiu, mo, mengbao* (ferocious leopard), and *shitieshou* (iron eating beast). *Pixiu* and *mo* are the names most commonly found, and research has shown that these creatures can only have been the modern Giant Panda.

The next day the men returned to the mountains, and since they had heard that Giant Pandas were drawn to the strong scent of mutton, they bought a sheep, which they killed, chopped and cooked. They eventually piqued the interest of an adult panda, and after rounding on the creature were able to subdue and cage it, before taking it down the mountain. It was at this time that Wang Haitang realized that the foreigners' intention to hunt the unicorn was fake, and the real object

Views of the Ganyang Valley (taken by Hou Xiaojun)

of their desire was the panda. Enraged, their host at once called over his men, who promptly ran the brothers out of town. Shanggan Valley was henceforth known as "Ganyang (expel foreigners) Valley."

More than half a century later, Wang Haitang's home is still standing, though it has long since fallen into disrepair; the wood cabin frequented by the Roosevelt sons is also still there, and today functions as a granary; Wang Haitang's de-

Wang Haizhen, granddaughter of the old landlord Wang Haitang, by the ancient watchtower

scendents are still around, living an unadorned, simple life in the new tile-roofed houses beside the old family home. Ganyang Valley, too, still endures, and has come to be a renowned tourist destination.

From the end of the nineteenth century through to the middle of the twentieth, Westerners heading to China to hunt Giant Pandas was still relatively common.

The German Schaefer Expedition on the grass slopes of the Qionglai Mountains in search of Giant Pandas in 1931

Between 1891 and 1894, two Russians were in Sichuan, where they bought a panda pelt which they shipped back to Russia. The specimen has been housed in the British Museum.

Between 1897 and 1935, three expeditions entered Sichuan, bringing back four Giant Panda specimens in total, which are on show at the British Museum.

In 1916, the German zoologist Weigold was able to capture a Giant Panda cub, marking the first time that a Westerner had caught a live panda. Sadly the cub died before it could be shipped abroad, and he had to make do with four Giant Panda skulls and pelts, which were housed in the Berlin Museum.

From 1926 to 1928, the Roosevelt sons visited Sichuan twice, killing six Giant Pandas which were taken as specimens for the Chicago Museum of Natural History.

In 1931, the Dolan expedition from the U.S. killed a Giant Panda in Sichuan and got two specimens. They were all housed at the Philidelphia Museum of Natural History.

In 1934, Sage and Sheldon, likewise members of the Dolan expedition, hunted and killed an adult Giant Panda, which was later housed in the American Museum of Natural History in New York.

Ruth and Sulin

Of the countless foreigners who went to China in search of Giant Pandas, the first to bring a live one out of the country was neither an explorer nor a zoologist, but rather a young fashion designer from America, Ruth Harkness. In 1936, Ruth's newly-wed husband William Harkness, a zoologist and explorer, arrived in China on the lookout for pandas. Tragically, he fell ill and died not long after his arrival. After rushing out to Shanghai to arrange

Ruth sends Sulin for a checkup

her husband's funeral, Ruth decided to finish what her husband had started—searching for Giant Pandas in the mountains.

Braving unimaginable hardship, Ruth trekked through miles unending forests before finally stumbling across a panda cub. Barely four weeks old and weighing less than three pounds, the cub was sighted with the help of a local hunter as it lay in the cavity of a tree. Ruth named the cub Sulin, and cared for it meticulously all the way back to Shanghai. By claiming Sulin to be a Pekinese dog, together with a two dollar bribe, Ruth was able to get the cub past customs officers and onto the President McKinlay steamer bound for San Francisco.

The vessel arrived at San Francisco on Christmas Eve, and a group of New York explorers laid on a lavish party for them. In the Spring of 1937, Sulin was exhibited at the Chicago Zoo, which drew a crowd of over forty thousand people on the opening day. Ruth and Sulin's story spread, and soon the Western world had become quite fascinated by the Giant Panda.

According to data, from 1869 to 1946 over two hundred foreigners went to China in search of Giant Pandas. From 1936 to 1941, nine live pandas were brought from China to the United States. In the mere ten year period from 1936 to 1946 no fewer than sixteen live pandas were brought out of China, as well as seventy specimens which were housed in overseas museums.

Chapter Three

Wuyi Shed, the Birthplace of Giant Panda Conservation

Baiyun: If the gunshots had continued to ring in the air, it's possible that we would have been killed off long ago. Luckily, humans woke up to the damage they were causing, and stopped the senseless killing. However, they did not completely forget about us, but rather focused their attention in a more positive way. They came to our natural habitat where they constructed observation stations, and watched how and where we lived. From that point on our solitary lives were no longer a secret...

When it was confirmed that Giant Pandas can be found only in the mountains of China, they became something of a national treasure for the Chinese. Giant Pandas' irresistible charm unsurprisingly made them China's gift of choice to other nations. From the 1950s to the 1980s, many a foreign leader came to China in the hope of returning home with a pair of Giant Pandas. The most famous case is that of President Nixon whose visit to China in 1972 began to thaw the chilly relations which had existed between China and the United States for over two decades. It was a pair of Giant Pandas, Lingling and Xingxing, who were the messengers of this new-found friendship, and upon their arrival in America another bout of "pandamonium" began to spread throughout the country.

But how many of China's treasured pandas were there, and would they be given away until none remained? In 1974, China undertook the first nationwide Giant Panda survey. Following the four-year study it was concluded that panda numbers within and without China barely exceeded 2,400, and the Giant Panda had become an endangered species...

In order to protect China's famed creatures, it was first necessary to understand the way they live. In March 1978, a young Chinese biologist braved the elements on his way to the Wolong Nature Reserve in the Minshan Mountains. He would

Wuyi Shed's towering trees as seen today

Professor Hu Jinchu

later become the authority on Giant Pandas, Professor Hu Jinchu. Professor Hu was not only in charge of the eight thousand-strong team who conducted the 4,500 kilometer-wide study, but during the study also pioneered the "Hu Method" for calculating Giant Panda numbers, which led to the smooth completion of the project. For this reason, the responsibility of establishing the observation station fell squarely on the the shoulders of Professor Hu.

The Minshan Mountain is dotted with high peaks, deep gulleys, and thick forests, an ideal place of Giant Panda activity. The Wolong Nature Reserve covers some twenty thousand hectares, and posesses ideal conditions for the conservation of Giant Pandas. Following local reconaissance, Professor Hu selected an area of gentle slopes 2,500 meters above sea level. After levelling the ground, setting up tents and digging a well, Professor Hu, along with his assistants and workers, had succeeded in establishing the world's first Giant Panda observation center—Wuyi Shed.

There are many accounts of how Wuyi (literally "five one") Shed got its name. Some state that it was completed on the May Day holiday, while others claim that there were five sheds... However, only the version told by Professor Hu can be believed, for it was the professor himself who coined the name. At that time, between the sleeping quarters to the well was a slope of fifty-one arduous steps. Thirty years on, the site has undergone a number of renovations, and is now both magnificent and fully-equipped, like a hidden villa among the forests. The fifty-one steps to the water well have long since disappeared, yet Wuyi Shed's name

A list of some of the early Giant Pandas donated to foreign nations

Pingping, An'an: Sent to the former Soviet Union in 1955 and 1958 respectively;
Number 1, Number 2, Lingling, Sanxing, Dandan: Sent to North Korea between 1965 and 1979;
Lingling, Xingxing: Sent to the United States in 1972;
Lanlan, Kangkang, Huanhuan, Feifei: Sent to Japan between 1972 and 1980;
Lili, Yanyan: Sent to France in 1974;
Jiajia, Jingjing: Sent to Britain in 1974;
Yingying, Beibei: Sent to Mexico in 1975.

The Wuyi Shed observation station of the 1990s

The 21st century Wuyi Shed observation station

has endured, reminding visitors of the harsh conditions which once existed there.

In 1980, the World Wildlife Fund (later renamed World Wildlife Fund for Nature) became the first international organization to use the Giant Panda as its logo. Together with another famous conservation organization IUCN (the International Union for Conservation of Nature), they came to China with the hope of

The WWF logo

cooperating with the Chinese government in the study of Giant Panda conservation. After a series of talks, both parties agreed to put forward a million dollars, which would be used to create the Wolong Giant Panda breeding center, and experts from both parties would work together in their research.

In December 1980, WWF and IUCN invited renowned ecology expert Professor George B. Schaller to Wuyi Shed, officially marking the start of the first international Giant Panda research project. The cooperative project was headed by two

The WWF logo

In 1961, a group of the world's scientists convened for the first time with the goal of establishing the World Wildlife Fund (now known as the World Wildlife Fund for Nature). At the time, a Giant Panda by the name of Jiji was being exhibited at London Zoo. The droves of people who turned out to see her gave the scientists a chance to witness the appeal of Giant Pandas, and it was for this reason that they chose to represent their organization using this now-familiar logo. Scottish naturalist Gerald Watterson drew up the earliest draft of the symbol, which the WWF's first chairman Peter Scott built upon in his creation of the WWF's first official logo. Forty years on, the symbol of the WWF has undergone several improvements, showing an ever-greater sense of style and uniqueness, and at the same time becoming the symbol of the conservation movement for people all over the world.

The cover of *Wolong's Giant Panda*

men, Professor Schaller from the foreign team and Professor Hu Jinchu from the Chinese team.

The arrival of Professor George B. Schaller brought with it a host of modern reasearch techniques, signalling a new era for Wuyi Shed's research. Using traps and tranquilizer guns to capture the animals and collars and wireless detectors to follow them, the team got a fix on six wild pandas for their research, which they named Zhenzhen, Weiwei, Pipi, Hanhan, Pingping and Kuikui.

Though these six pandas are no more, their eating and sleeping habits, varying moods, ageing and finally deaths were all charted between 1980 and 1985, providing their researchers with a wealth of knowledge. In 1985 came the first fruit of the international project, in the form of the world's first in-depth volume on the state of Giant Pandas in the wild, *Wolong's Giant Panda*, was published in China. In 1992, George B. Schaller's *The Last Panda* was published in America. The work was based on his own diary entries during his time at Wuyi Shed.

Chapter Four

Wolong, the Cradle of Artificial Breeding

Baiyun: Wolong (literally "resting dragon"), my hometown which I hold so dear, has filled my dreams ever since I left. Legend has it that long, long ago a dragon was flying past the mountains. He immediately fell for the green hills and clear waters, and after descending through the clouds, rested on the hills and has yet to leave. It seems that people too fell for the region, leading them to build Wuyi Shed and eventually the Wolong Giant Panda Breeding Center. But thriving in the man-made conditions so different from the free, wild environment which previous generations enjoyed has been no easy task...

From 1980 to 1990, the WWF and IUCN together with the Chinese government set up China's Wolong Giant Panda Breeding Center, complete with houses, generators, and new roads, yet in that time not a single Giant Panda cub was born. With mounting international pressure as well as doubts from within China, many wondered whether the maligned breeding center had any future.

At that time, China's 1985–1989 Giant Panda study had already been completed, which showed Giant Panda numbers to have shrunk from 2,400 in the first study to just 1,100. Because of this, the Chinese government once more joined forces with the WWF, drawing up their "Plans for the Conservation of the Giant Panda and its Habitat" which would later become the Giant Panda Conservation Project.

The team in charge of the Giant Panda Conservation Project that Giant Panda conservation comprised of two elements. Firstly, the expansion of their natural habitat, ensuring survival and diversity across the species, and secondly by upping the pace of artificial breeding, both satisfying the demands of an awaiting public and paving the way for Giant Pandas to eventually return to the wild. Kickstarting the Wolong Giant Panda Breeding Center was now the Giant Panda Conservation Project's top priority.

Siguniang Mountain, the main peak of the Qionglai Mountains

Strong and virile Giant Pandas from all around the country were deployed, and experts with experience in Giant Panda breeding from Beijing were sent in, along with 150,000 Chinese *yuan* each year for three years, by the end of which time the project would be abandoned if success was not forthcoming. These were the conditions that were both laid down by the Giant Panda Conservation Project, and promised by the Wolong Center.

Just after Spring Festival in 1991, Beijing Zoo's resident expert Liu Weixin arrived at the Wolong Center. Beijing Zoo played host to the first natural Giant Panda birth in captivity with the birth of Mingming in 1962, and in 1978, the world's first Giant Panda birth through artificial insemination occured when twin cubs Yuanjing and Kaiyuan were born under the supervision of a team led by none other than Liu Weixin.

In Wolong, the research team selected Panpan and Dongdong, a pair of pandas from the Qionglai Mountains as their targets for artificial breeding. Panpan was a tall, strapping six-year-old male, while Dongdong was a docile, attractive female, and the pair fell for each other immediately.

On September 7th 1991, following the birth of two adorable cubs Baiyun and Lüdi, the Wolong National Giant Panda Breeding Center had reaped its first rewards. However, Lüdi was rejected by his mother, and despite artificial rearing lived just 159 days. This setback left an indelible mark in the hearts of the Wolong team, and spurred them on in their continued efforts.

China's main Giant Panda breeding grounds

Beijing Zoo: Ever since Giant Panda feeding programmes were introduced more than fifty years ago in 1955, Beijing Zoo has been the earliest zoo in China to exhibit pandas reared and bred in captivity. From its first breeding success in 1963 until 2006, the zoo had 40 pregnancies and 65 offspring, of which 32 survived. At the same time, Beijing Zoo's committed research into Giant Panda breeding, nutrition, disease, dissection and inherited traits has also seen a number of important breakthroughs. The Giant Panda area of the zoo covers 12,605 square meters.

National Panda Conservation Research Center: Located in Sichuan Province's Wolong, the center has creatively solved three great problems in panda breeding, namely the problem of heat, problem of mating, and problem of rearing, thanks to more than twenty years of hard work. From 1999 until 2005, the center's survival rate for cubs stood at 100% each year. In 2003, the Ya'an Bifeng Gorge Base was established, sensibly providing a secondary site for Giant Pandas. Until the end of 2005, the center was responsible for 95 Giant Panda births, the largest figure for captively-bred pandas in the world.

Chengdu Giant Panda Breeding Research Base: Covering some 35.5 hectares, and resting on

Panpan at the Bifeng Gorge Base in 2005

From 1991 until 2000, the Wolong Giant Panda Breeding Center was in its second decade, and it was a decade of great success. In ten short years the Wolong team was able to overcome three major hurdles in Giant Panda breeding.

The first of these hurdles was the problem of going into heat. It had been observed that of those Giant Pandas raised in captivity, 30% of females either did not go into heat at all, or did not reach their peak. Experts had a number of differing opinions on why this was the case. Some believed that it was a change in diet, some pointed to a difference in environment, while others believed that females lacked contact with the scents of other males, and yet more saw the lack of early behavioral learning as the root of the problem. In response, the Wolong team started a number of trials: improve the Giant Pandas' nutrition by introducing supplements into their diet; changing their enclosures to increase female and male contact; giving developing females a chance to

Futou Mountain ten kilometers to the north of Chengdu City, the research base is currently home to 47 Giant Pandas. In 1997 an open research laboratory was completed, underlining its commitment to reproductive biology, conservation genetics, endocrinology and ecology.

Shaanxi Wild Animal Rescue and Research Center: Situated in Shaanxi Province's Zhouzhi County, the center, which was established in 2001, now covers 104.7 hectares. To date the center has rescued 36 wild Giant Pandas. Current facilities include a Giant Panda enclosure and play area of some 15,000 square meters, where over ten pandas have been raised. In 2003 the center celebrated its first artificially-bred cub.

Innocent playmates

Stop crowding me!

Delicious

Enjoying bamboo shoots

Dinner time

The outside world

study Giant Panda behavior by showing videos of adult pandas' mating. After exhaustive study, researchers were finally able to improve the situation.

The second problem was one of impregnation. Giant Pandas are in heat for a very short period of time, typically just two to five days each year, and after longterm observation looking at both their hormones and behaviors, experts were able to correctly predict when pandas came into heat, expediating natural mating as well as artificial insemination, which greatly increased the rate of successful impregnation.

The third hurdle was the problem of rearing young. After close observation it was discovered that Giant Panda breast milk contained irreplaceable anti-immune agents, meaning that access to their mother's milk was a case of life and death for young cubs. Yet the rejection of cubs observed in Giant Pandas inevitably stopped cubs from receiving their mother's milk. The team were forced to use somewhat underhand methods, allowing the two cubs to

Yuanjing with its mother Juanjuan (provided by Liu Weixin)

Firsts in Giant Panda artificial breeding

First birth in captivity: In September 1963, Giant Pandas Pipi and Lili, both from Beijing Zoo, bred naturally to produce their cub Mingming. This was the world's first captively-bred Giant Panda.

First success through artificial insemination: In 1978, Beijing Zoo used the fresh sperm of Loulou and Baobao to artificially inseminate Juanjuan, resulting in the birth of Yuanjing. This was the first successful artificial insemination of a Giant Panda using fresh sperm.

First artificial insemination using frozen sperm: In 1980, Beijing Zoo used Baobao's frozen sperm to artificially inseminate Daidai, resulting in the birth of twin cubs. This represents the world's first Giant Panda insemination using frozen sperm.

First triplets: In September 1967, Shanghai Zoo's Giant Panda Jingji gave birth to triplets. This was the first artificially-bred case of Giant Panda triplets in history.

First man-aided rearing of twin cubs: In August 1990, Qingqing from Chengdu Zoo gave birth to twins Yaya and Junjun, who were reared to adulthood with the help of man, the first such case in history.

The first fully artificial rearing of twin cubs: In September 1992, Beijing Zoo's Yongyong gave birth to a pair of twins, Yongming and Yongliang. After being rejected by his mother, Yongliang had to be fully reared by hand. This was the world's first case of fully artificial rearing of a twin cub.

The oldest mother: In July 2002, Xinxing from Chongqing Zoo gave birth to twins at the age of twenty, making her the oldest Giant Panda mother in history.

feed one after another when the mother was asleep, ensuring that their intake was sufficient. At the same time, they also worked hard to improve their care of the young offspring, as well as their rearing environment. This two-tiered approach greatly increased the survival rates of young Giant Panda cubs.

The year 2000 was one of great celebration for the Wolong Center. That year, no fewer than twelve cubs were born, all of whom survived infancy, marking the start of a tradition which would continue on. In the preceeding ten years the Wolong Center had not only focused on the plight of the pandas, but also carefully fostered their own team of experts, including Zhang Hemin, Wang Pengyan, Zhang Guiquan and Wei Rongping. In the 1980s they had just graduated from university, at that time working as green yet eager assistants to Professor Hu Jinchu; a decade on and their grounding and hard work gave them a wealth of experience under the tutelage of Liu Weixin; stepping into the 21st century, these mature and brilliant men had not only become experts on Giant Panda breeding in their own right, but also exceeded the achievements of their predecessors, making the Wolong Center home to more than half of all Giant Pandas in captivity, and helping the Giant Panda as a species in a way that will be celebrated forever.

From the year 2000 onwards, the Wolong Center has had at least ten Giant Panda cubs each year including twins and triplets, and virtually all have gone on to survive into adulthood. The highest figure for a single year is sixteen cubs. In order to provide even better care for the cubs, the Wolong Center has established a panda kindergarten.

Looking at happy, boisterous young panda cubs playing in the panda kindergarten, one must think of Baiyun in America. If she had not been born, the Wolong Center we know today would not have been. We must think, too, of poor Lüdi, whose desperate but ultimately unsuccessful fight for life has remained in people's hearts and minds...

Putting pandas first

"Putting pandas first" is the motto of the Wolong Giant Panda Breeding Center. Since pandas in the wild are on the lookout for food 24 hours a day, the Wolong Center have introduced the idea of the "24 hour panda," whereby three square meals a day have been abandoned in favour of a number of feeding times spaced throughout the day and night. Moreover, during mating season wild pandas are free to find their own mates, so the team mix male and female pandas in Spring; wild pandas must search for their food, so the team intentionally hide food for the pandas to find; Giant Pandas in the wild typically give birth in tree cavities or caves, and so cavity-filled trees are brought into the enclosures; since panda mothers display rejecting behavior, they swap the rejected offspring for the accepted one while the mother is asleep. In other words, at the Wolong Center they try their utmost to satisfy the pandas' needs according to their natural habits, in a policy which has been dubbed "putting pandas first."

Chapter Five

Lüdi, My Poor, Brave Brother

Baiyun: Time really flies, and today I am the mother of five sons and daughters. Each time a new cub is born, I can't help but think of Lüdi, who would have children of his own were he still alive. Though he is my brother, I never got to see him. I was also denied the chance to hear his voice, which they say was resounding and shrill. At the time I too had just come into the world and could only suckle my mother, eyes still closed and hearing still undeveloped. When I grew up I heard that I had a twin brother named Lüdi who was rejected by our mother and fed by humans. Though his life spanned just 159 short days, each one left an indelible impression on all who knew him...

On September 7th 1991, Panpan and Dongdong's twin cubs were born in the Wolong Center. First to be born was their daughter Baiyun. Dongdong adored her daughter, one moment hugging her close, the next holding her in her mouth, but never letting her go. Soon after came Lüdi, yet Dongdong refused to acknowledge him, leaving him to crawl and yelp on the ground alone...

According to experts, this was Giant Panda "rejection" behavior. In the wild, owing to the difficult conditions, reliance on bamboo, lack of adequate nutrition, and an ability to only feed one cub at a time, if a mother tries to keep both cubs, it is possible that neither will survive, so female Giant Pandas must make this difficult choice.

However, Lüdi was unwilling to give up. Still wet from the amniotic fluid and with the umbilical cord attached, he blindly struggled to himself up. Lifting his head, Lüdi began to crawl along the cold floor letting out a shrill cry as he moved, begging for his mother's precious milk.

An hour had passed, and the Wolong team were praying for Dongdong to accept her poor child. Yet Dongdong was still quite impassive. Another hour rolled on, and Lüdi was no longer able to crawl, his cries now muted. The team were still waiting, imploring Dongdong to take in her exhausted cub.

Dongdong once again paid him no heed.

Lüdi's breathing had become weak, and the team could not bear to see the poor cub perish. Yet panda cubs are not human babies, and with all the will in the world, there was nothing that humans could do for him. Even expert Liu Weixin who had been brought over from Beijing Zoo had no answer to the problem. Previously, scientists had tried many times, each ending in heartbreaking failure:

In 1978, Kaiyuan was artificially reared at Beijing Zoo, dying after two days.

In 1982, the newborn cub was artificially reared and died after just three day at Madrid Zoo.

In 1985, the abandoned cub died after two days at Mexico Zoo.

From 1987 onwards, Kunming Zoo and Chengdu Zoo artificially reared a number of Giant Panda cubs, none living beyond 25 days.

Since 1980, Beijing Zoo has set up a team to address the issue of artificial rearing. However, until the birth of Lüdi in 1990, the longest an artificially-reared cub had survived was just 75 days.

By this time scientists had already discovered that the answer to panda cubs' survival lay in their mothers' milk. Panda breast milk contains vital nutrients which artificial milk lacks, which can boost the cub's immune system and improve its chance of survival. To address this, expert Liu Weixin looked into synthesizing artificial milk using fresh cows' milk, ground crab, vitamins, calcium and most importantly proteins which boost immunity. Time was needed to establish whether the ingredients and proportions would have the desired effect.

Yet Lüdi could not afford to wait. He was already nearing death, and the team immediately took him out using a long pole with a string bag and placed him into a warming chamber where he was fed the artificial milk. Lüdi was observed round the clock, and the formula was adjusted according to his condition.

The abandoned Lüdi persevered and struggled along with the Wolong team, valiantly fighting for his life at every stage. Below is a record of his early days:

September 7th: Lüdi was born a healthy 137

Rejecting behavior of Giant Pandas

After the Fourth Ice Age, the Giant Panda species transformed its diet from one of meat to one centered around bamboo, a change which had a detrimental effect on their nutrition. For this reason, Giant Panda mothers in the wild predominantly produce just one cub, and even if they have twins, are only able to rear one, being faced with the choice of abandoning one or losing both. The man-made conditions and breeding techniques for pandas in captivity mean that today Giant Pandas frequently give birth to two or even three cubs in one litter, all of which can be reared to adulthood.

The captive Giant Panda population

From 1963 until 1987, the foundation for the artificial breeding of Giant Pandas came from the breeding of animals captured or saved from the wild. 1988 until 1997 saw a sharp increase in the numbers of later-generation Giant Pandas bred artificially. In 1997, the number of Giant Pandas in captivity was higher than in the wild for the first time in history. From 1998 until 2005, artificially-bred pandas gradually replaced animals rescued from the wild, comprising the core of those kept in captivity. Currently, the population of artificially-bred Giant Pandas is more or less self sustaining.

grams, though was unable to get any milk for three hours. It had its first bowel movement four hours later. (A blessing.)

September 8th: Patches of baby fur started to appear, but due to improper feeding, Lüdi choked over his milk and his weight dropped to 129 grams. (Things were not encouraging.)

September 9th: His dried umbilical cord fell off, and his movement and cries became somewhat weaker. His weight dropped to a perilous 106 grams. (He was dying.)

September 10th: Lüdi's movement and cries became weaker still as he suffered extreme exhaustion and dejection. (Take measures!)

September 11th: His condition improved somewhat, his intake of milk increased, and his weight stood at 97.5 grams. (He was saved from the jaws of death.)

September 12th: Lüdi's condition showed further improvement, his weight increased to 103 grams, and he lost his baby fur. (Thank goodness!)

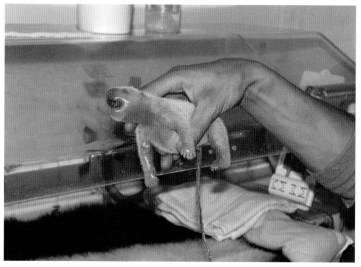

Lüdi at birth (taken by Zhang Guiquan)

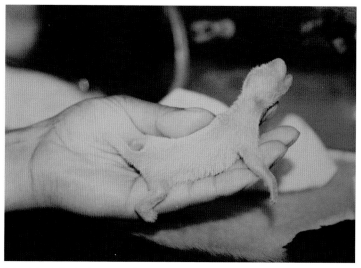

Lüdi at 2 days (taken by Zhang Guiquan)

Lüdi at 15 days (taken by Zhang Guiquan)

Lüdi at 25 days (taken by Zhang Guiquan)

Lüdi at 2 months (taken by Zhang Guiquan)

Lüdi at 5 months (taken by Zhang Guiquan)

Giant Panda communication

Giant Pandas have a highly complex system of communication, with cries varying in not only volume but also length. Adult Giant Pandas have eleven distinct cries: bleating, tweeting, moaning, barking, howling, yelping, lowing, smacking, puffing, snorting, and roaring. These can be divided into four types of signal. Bleating and tweeting are signs of high spirits; barking and yelping are signs of mildly threatening behavior; howling and roaring are used when an individual is poised to attack; puffing, snorting, and smacking are all signs of fear. Of the eleven calls, more than half are related to mating, these being bleating, tweeting, barking, howling, yelping and roaring.

September 13th: His condition stabilized, and his ears, eyes, limbs and shoulders showed faint grey markings. His weight stood at 105 grams. (Growing well.)

September 14th: His food intake had increased, his dark patches became more pronounced, and his weight increased to 115.5 grams. (Happily encouraged.)

September 15th: At 8 am, he ran into problems when the milk entered his windpipe. For six hours his condition worsened, and he was unable to drink milk or let out cries, and for ten long hours was left twitching and breathing with difficulty. (Oxygen therapy immediately.)

September 16th: At 00:30 at midnight he finally let out a cry. He was also able to start drinking milk. (A turn for the better.)

September 17th: His food intake increased, his bowel movements became normal, and his weight improved to 111.5 grams. (He survived.)

September 18th: The area around his ears and eyes became black and his weight increased to 123.5 grams. (How lovely!)

Sepember 19ᵗʰ: All his black markings appeared, his claws began to grow rapidly, and his weight increased to 132.8 grams. (Bravo!)

September 20ᵗʰ: Murmurs could be heard in his chest. His appetite was not as good as before, but his weight increased to 135 grams. (Oxygen therapy again.)

September 21ˢᵗ: Respiratory murmurs continued, and his weight dipped to 126 grams. (Hold out, Lüdi!)

September 22ⁿᵈ: He was given Oxygen therapy at intervals. His appetite improved, and his weight increased to 132.5 grams. (We made it again.)

September 23ʳᵈ: His appetite had returned to normal, oxygen therapy continued, and his weight increased to 153 grams, the first time it had been above his birth weight. (We were wild with joy.)

So it went, each day and night filled with hope and despair, as Lüdi bravely clung on for survival. The days, weeks and months went by, and for one, two, three, four, five months, both Lüdi and the Wolong team refused to give in.

However, on day 159, Lüdi passed away, officially due to "heart failure caused by pneumonia and emphysema."

Lüdi lived for less than six months, yet broke the record

Liu Weixin with Yongming and Yongliang (provided by Liu Weixin)

for a panda cub reared artificially. Though Lüdi had gone, his brave struggle for life etched an idea indelibly in people's minds: Every creature is reluctant to let go of life, and will fight for it no matter their plight. There is splendor in every battle, and each day is another victory. This is what it means to live.

In the Autumn of Lüdi's death, Beijing Zoo celebrated another set of twins, the younger of which was also abandoned by his mother. This time, however. Liu Weixin who had by then returned back from Wolong was able to rear the cub to health himself, writing a new chapter in the history of artificially reared Giant Panda cubs.

Chapter Six

Fate, the Story behind the Names

Baiyun: Ever since we were discovered by a French priest in Baoxing, we have been referred to collectively as "Giant Pandas." Since Ruth Harkness gave her panda the name Sulin, each of us who has entered the human society has a name of our own. Initially, our names were decided by one or two people, yet later these decisions became regional and national ones. The largest decision-making process was that for Tuantuan and Yuanyuan, in which more than 100 million people took part. Each name represents mankind's hopes, and each carries with it a story all its own...

Lingling

It is well known that the cold standoff between China and America began to thaw back in 1972, when Chairman Mao and President Nixon famously shook hands at Zhongnanhai. What is less well known, however, is that 1972 was referred to by many Americans as "Panda Year." This can be put down to two Giant Pandas, Lingling and Xingxing. During Henry Kissinger's secret visit to China that year, he not only discussed political matters, but also made a special request: that two Giant Pandas be sent to the United States.

Lingling was born in Sichuan, and the early book *Baoxing Pandas* gives the following description:

The Giant Panda Lingling's home is Mahuang Valley, lying below Jiajin Mountain, a site which the Red Army marched through ever before. In September 1971, a member of staff at the wild animal capture station established by Beijing Zoo in Lianghekou, chanced upon a lumbering Giant Panda during his patrol of the Mahuang Valley. Upon being spotted the panda dashed off, leaving a cub behind. Wang Xingtai picked the animal up and put it into his winter hat, and took it back to the station. The cub weighed a mere 1.3 kilograms. From then on, the cub and Mr Wang were inseparable. When it reached the age of six months, because of the careful rearing of the workers, the ani-

mal's fur was as glistening and brilliant as a tiny jade buddha, which is how he got the name Lingling ("exquisite jade").

On April 16th 1976 Lingling and Xingxing were sent to Washington D.C. At the time, Lingling, still shy of her first birthday, weighed 61.8 kilograms.

Like the legend of Wang Zhaojun (lady-in-waiting at the Western Han court who volunteered to marry the chief of Xiongnu in the border areas in 33 BC), Lingling and Xingxing's fate was decided for them, yet instead of the harsh frontier, they were sent to the modern world of America.

Gaogao

In August 2009, Gaogao of San Diego Zoo once more became a father. Gaogao was sent to America in January 2003, specially selected to be Baiyun's mate. The two pandas really clicked, and that year they had Meisheng, followed by Sulin, Zhenzhen and Yunzi. The Associated Press once wrote an article in which they humorously referred to "the seed-sowing expert Gaogao."

In his youth Gaogao was an extremely strong and powerful specimen. His fur was not white but flaxen in color, both thick and hard, sticking out like a suit of armour. His spirited head

Gaogao at Wolong in 2002 (taken by Zhang Guiquan)

was more like that of a dog than the cat-like features typical of Giant Pandas.

Gaogao was well-known from an early age. There was an international prizewinning documentary made about Gaogao's life entitled *Returning Home*. The documentary recounts his life as follows:

In the Spring of 1993, Gaogao was sick in the wilderness, and was sent to the Nature Reserve by locals. By the look of him he was a mere six months old cub in need of his mother.

By the Winter of 1994, Gaogao had just turned two, and the round-headed, fiery-eyed cub was now sleeping soundly in his own cabin. Gaogao has a large appetite, and loved nothing more than rolling around in the snow, the very picture of a mischievous young boy.

That same Winter, the snow-filled yard was shrouded in a nighttime mist, and Gaogao's keeper Yang was training Gaogao to sleep up the tree. Yang would first carry the cub to the trunk, before patting him on the behind and shouting "up you go!"

Gaogao would begin his ascent before sitting on the crotch of the tree and looking at his keeper.

Yang headed to the entrance of the yard, buried in thick trees, with Gaogao in tow.

The keeper turned around, carrying Gaogao back to the bottom of the large tree, patting him again and imploring the young panda to return to the treetops: "Stay up there and do not come down, or you'll be eaten if you're not careful."

Gaogao duly complied. Once more Yang turned round to leave. He went a short distance, once more hid in the thick trees, and looked back. The trouble-making young cub was sitting in the tree, head turned, eyes blinking and ears pricked, anxiously awaiting nightfall. This was to be Gaogao's first night in the open, as Yang coldly locked the yard on his way out.

The next day, dawn was just breaking as Yang went to check on Gaogao. The young panda was lying in the bamboo trees, and as

The Fengtong Valley Nature Reserve Giant Panda keeper Li Wuke

he spotted his keeper, Gaogao rushed up to him, wearing a weary and unhappy expression on his face. Yang felt bad, and he patted the snow off Gaogao's head, returning him to his enclosure. Soon some steaming rice porridge was brought out, and Gaogao hungrily wolfed down the hot meal.

In the Spring of 1995, a team from the nature reserve made up of Yang Benqing, Yang Wenfu, Wang Bangjun and Li Wuke were examining the forests, streams and shrubs of the Qingshan Valley. This was the very heart of the nature reserve, with barely a trace of human life, and it was here that Gaogao was to be brought to live once more in the wild.

There was a poetic beauty to the scene, with blue skies, white clouds, green mountains and lush bamboo. Li Wuke was with his granddaughter, cutting down ripe bamboo. Dewdrops fell off the trees as Li Wuke tied the bamboo together, which he then carried on his back.

The granddaughter, dressed in red and bounding along behind, let out a merry folk song as she went:

To Qingshan Valley went a lad,
No better bamboo can be had

Shortly before Gaogao's departure, a birthday party was held for the young panda. According to the tradition of the nature reserve, the date of rescue is celebrated as the animal's birthday. In the case of Gaogao, April 6th 1995 was his second birthday. A large, round sweetcorn cake was laid on, including two "candles" fashioned from peeled sugarcane sticks. A few flowers and a "Happy Birthday Gaogao!" message had also been written in cream on the cake, sending Gaogao off in style.

The naughty birthday boy finally sat down, taking a bite of the sweet "candles," and grabbing a handful of cream which ended up smeared across his face. He then took some cake which was stuffed greedily into the young panda's mouth. The workers began to laugh at the scene, and several local children were running around behind them.

"Come and take a photo with Gaogao," they told the children. "Sing him a song!"

Voices high and low joined in unison, as they all sang "Happy Birthday" to the cub.

On April 26th 1995, the skies were sunny and clear. Gaogao was really going. The keepers had been kept busy since early that morning. Two extra eggs were added to his rice porridge, for the panda would no longer be able to enjoy such treats. More tender bamboo was put in his enclosure, for he would no longer be reliant on his keepers for food. The keepers combed his hair with their fingers, imploring him to eat more, for this was his final feed. They then used a towel to clean Gaogao's fur in preparation for his return home. Gaogao was loaded into a Mitsubishi, as they made the drive to Qingshan Valley. The local farmers, wearing blue clothes and blue headpiece, looked on at the car as it went, shouting in their thick Sichuan accents: "What have you done with him? He looks great!"

Raised perilously on a shaky suspension bridge above a deep stream and flanked by steep slopes, the sedan chair was hoisted up, and Gaogao was taken up the mountain.

Gaogao then feasted on red apples, white sugarcane, and yellow steamed bread until he was quite full, by which time he was lying on the ground unwilling to move. He was prodded and shaken by the workers: "Get up! It's nearly dark." they implored. This time Gaogao really did go, lumbering forward as his round rear end wiggled with every step. Gaogao was gone, and as he disappeared among the redwood forests, the last faint glint of his fiery eyes could just be made out. He was gone, and took with him the love and attention of those who knew him:

"Will we ever see him again?" mused Yang.

"Sure we will. He's only going to be on one mountain." said Wang Bangjun.

"Will we recognize him?"

"Sure we will. He's got a bit missing from his ear."

Gaogao had finally returned home, and the movie ended with Li Wuke's folk song:

To Qingshan Valley went a lad,
No better bamboo can be had.

This was a fitting end to the story. Yet not long after, Gaogao once more returned to the Fengtong Valley Nature Reserve. From there he was sent to Wolong and, later, the United States of America.

For Gaogao, China is his home when he is in the U.S., while in China, Wolong and Fengtong Valley are his home. Yet his true home will always remain the Qionglai Mountains. Who could have known that after being brough to the Fengtong Valley, Gaogao's journey would take him all over the world?

Qingqing

When Qingqing died from ill health at the age of 9 on July 17th 2008, people could scarcely believe the news.

Qingqing was born in the Autumn of 1999 at the Wolong

Center. As the son of Dadi, grandson of Panpan, and nephew of Baiyun, Qingqing's was a proud and famous lineage. Qingqing was named by none other than the former Chinese Premier Zhu Ronggji. However, Qingqing's fame came primarily from his four attempted escapes.

At the age of three, still not yet an adult, Qingqing lived along with other young males the same age in the same enclosure at the Wolong Center. The area was rather small, and no matter which way he turned there was no way out; the steel fences were high, and climbing out was impossible. Everyday Qingqing circled the enclosure, looking through the cage and

Qingqing at the Bifeng Gorge Base in 2005

trying to fathom a way out.

That day, Qingqing called another male over towards the fence: "On your knees!"

The cub duly knelt, and Qingqing climbed on his back: "Stand up!"

The young male complied, and Qingqing stretch his way upwards: "Stand still!"

The cub stood still, and as Qingqing raised his legs, was able to climb over the enclosure walls.

Qingqing had escaped! The Wolong Center was in a state of chaos, and it took considerable effort to get Qingqing back home. From then on, the young cub was regarded in a new light.

At age four, Qingqing arrived at the Bifeng Gorge Base. The expansive skies and vast wilderness are a veritable playground of nature, especially for the young. Climbing steep slopes, rolling down hills, scaling trees, frolicking in the waters, the region is perfect for all manner of exercise.

One day, the keepers were cleaning out the yard, with Qingqing safely locked inside the panda hut. The keeper was not yet finished, the door was still locked, and Qingqing was growing impatient. He let out a cry, yet the door would still not open. He lost his temper, yet no one payed him any attention. With nobody willing to help, Qingqing had to take matters into his own hands...

He grabbed the steel fence and gave it a tug. It started to shake. A good sign...

He tugged it more forcefully. It shook even more. No problem!

With all his might, Qingqing gave one final tug, the force of which sent the lock crashing to the ground.

Qingqing had escaped again! The Bifeng team gave chase, and once more the troublesome animal was brought back.

One year later, and Qingqing was a young adult. He had become even more boisterous, and his legs were yet more agile. As to what was going on inside his head, nobody could tell.

One day strong winds and beating rain swept through the valley, shrouding the entire area in darkness. Every creature, both panda and human, was hiding in their rooms. Everyone except Qingqing, who remained in the yard unperturbed, walking around and keeping an eye out. He trembled as water dripped down his back, yet seemed even more energetic. The harsh winds hit his eyes, yet his stare was more penetrating than ever.

The team were curious: What is he doing there? What is he waiting for?

Qingqing flashed them a look: "I'm not telling you," it seemed to say.

Just then, an old tree which had been rocking in the wind fell with a thud. Just what Qingqing had been looking for!

This shaky "bridge" was perched along the enclosure wall, just waiting for Qingqing.

Seizing his opportunity, Qingqing did not hesitate for a moment. Braving the wind and rain, he crossed the bridge, and with a short sprint climed over the fence to freedom.

Qingqing had escaped for the third time! The Bifeng team were astounded at the intelligence and craftiness of this young panda.

At age six, Qingqing had grown to become both dashing and playful, though sadly his desire to escape still remained. This time escape depended not on fortune nor friends, but on him alone. With hands gripping the wall, and feet on the ground, Qingqing summoned all his energy to leap up and over the enclosure walls. He passed Baixiong Fields and Baozi Hill, exploring houses and kitchens for anything to eat. He ran after tourists, who fled in panic. He chased other pandas who cried with fright. Yet Qingqing remained defiant: "run and cry all you want," he seemed to be saying, "I can run further and cry louder than all of you!"

Eventually Qingqing had run far enough, and was once again captured and brought back to his enclosure. This time, the team watched his every move. The walls were made higher, the fences were made thicker, visitors were prohibited, and even the keepers stayed well away, leaving Qingqing in a yard with only one way in and out.

If Qingqing's strength and might came from his father Dadi, his predilection for escape was surely inherited from his mother Baixue. In the Giant Panda circle, her escapology was known to all.

Baixue hailed from the heart of the Qinling Mountains, and was sent to the Shaanxi Wild Animal Rescue and Research Center in 1993. Less than a year later, while being exhibited at the Suzhou Fangshan National Park, she took the park staff off guard and dashed out of her enclosure, before hiding amongst the thick trees of the forest. She was only found and returned a full 38 days after her escape. In 1995, the now grown up Baixue was loaned to the Wolong Center, with the intention of mating and breeding. Yet in Spring 2001, two years after the birth of Qingqing, Baixue once more evaded her keepers, opening the lock and dashing for freedom. Baixue remained in hiding for four and a half years, until the Winter of 2005 when she was brought back to Wolong. In that long stretch of time, she doubtless found a mate in the wild, leaving a legacy of bright youngsters behind her.

Qingqing left behind a daughter, also named Qingqing. It remains to be seen whether she has inherited her father and grandmother's irrepressible urge for freedom.

Baiyang (literally "white poplar")

On March 7th 2005, two members of the Jiajin Mountain's Forestry Administration were on patrol in Baoxing County's Baiyangpeng, when they discovered Giant Panda footprints in a thick pile of snow. They followed the tracks, which led them to a Giant Panda cub no older than four or five months, who was huddled up on a white poplar tree, not moving a muscle. They were careful not to disturb the creature, for it was possible that the tracks they had found belonged to the cub's mother, who might well return soon to feed her cub. Yet after two days, the cub was still up the tree, his mother still out of sight. If the situation remained the same, the young panda cub would surely starve, and so it was decided that the cub should be taken in and sent to the Fengtong Valley Nature Reserve to live in a small, muddy yard.

There was a three-meter tall barren tree trunk in the yard, which Baiyang climbed the moment he arrived. Clinging onto

Baoxing County from afar

the bare branches and keeping quite motionless, Baiyang would stay there day and night, descending only to eat, clearly in a state of depression.

The keeper Ma Hong arrived with a bowl of milk, at which point Baiyang finally climbed down. However, after finishing the milk and licking the bowl clean, he once more made his way up the tree and refused to move. Ma Hong confirmed that the cub had behaving this way ever since his arrival, suggesting that the cub still missed his mother.

According to experts, adult Giant Pandas very rarely fall victim to accidents of nature, for their claws and teeth are both

An unhappy Baiyang in 2005

exceedingly sharp. When confronted by jackals, leopards or such like, they stand with their back to a tree or rock face, and no animal is willing to take its chances. However, four-month-

Baiyang as an adult in 2006

old cubs have yet to develop sharp teeth and claws, and defending themselves is therefore a real problem. For this reason, when mothers go off in search of food they make sure to hide their young in the thick trees, out of danger until they return. They will also rush back as quickly as possible to feed their cubs having satisfied their own appetites. Yet Baiyang's mother had not returned for two days, so it is quite probable that something had indeed happened to her.

Clearly, little Baiyang had listened well when his mother instructed him to wait atop the tree until her return. Little did the poor creature know that he would never again see her again.

Entrance to the Fengtong Valley Nature Reserve

Workers at the Fengtong Valley Nature Reserve return from their patrol of the mountains

In 2006 Baiyang was sent to the Bifeng Gorge Base, where he still liked to wait up trees. He would even scale trees eight or nine meters in height, from which he would stare out into the distance. After his first birthday, Baiyang's feeder Dong Li confirmed that the cub had become far more active than before, sometimes even venturing down to the ground to play.

Having eaten the milk or cornbread given to him by his feeders, Baiyang would not immediately return to the treetop, but would instead stick around to play with the tyre in his enclosure, which he would sit on, fall off, crawl into, throw around, or carry on his shoulders, in a state of happiness and concentration clearly visible in his proud face. However, after a while, he would fall into his familiar pattern of climbing the tops of the highest trees and looking out longingly. No matter how old he got or how much time passed, Baiyang could never get his mother's instructions out of his head, still awaiting patiently for her return. Since Baiyang was able to grow up healthily, the best thing was to let him wait up the tree, keeping his futile yet beautiful hopes alive.

Lele

It is said that in the 1970s and '80s the Qionglai Mountains were home to a farmer by the name of Wang Quan'an. He lived alone in a wooden cabin deep in the mountains, with no neighbors for miles. If he wanted to visit a friend or buy necessities, he would have to tramp over hill and dale for several miles, either to Fengtong Valley, or a little further to Baoxing County.

Mr Wang was poor and undemanding in his lifestyle: his wooden hut leaked; wind frequently whistled through the door; the roof was riddled with holes; his clothes were patched up; the bedding was old; bowls were chipped and pots rusted. Yet Mr Wang thought himself fortunate. He was able to grow his own food, he kept pigs and chickens, and could keep up with local news when visiting town to buy odds and ends or repair his clothes. In short, Wang Quan'an was both comfortable and content.

Shortly before Spring Festival in 1981, Mr Wang was on his way back from Baoxing County where he had gone to buy Spring Festival goods. Wang and his family were all hoping for a good year. They had just given offerings to the kitchen god, yet were shocked to find that in the night their entire stock of Spring Festival food had been stolen. Not one piece of fruit, pastry or meat had been left. Bits and pieces were strewn all over the floor, and not only was the food gone, but also pot lids, wooden bowls and ladles.

Who could have done such a thing? It certainly was not a

human, for nobody would travel several miles to steal such inexpensive goods. It must have been an animal. Yet this animal only stole food, and did not attack anyone, which ruled out tigers, leopards and wolves. It must have been a wild boar!

That evening, the entire family hid inside the hut, armed with sticks and kitchen knives, awaiting the beast's arrival. "You ate our meat," they thought, "so it's our turn to eat yours." By the time it got dark, the creature returned once more. It was big, swaying about and quite calm, looking very much at home. "If we can take him down we'll be well fed for the year," they all thought. Yet as it came close, Wang got a clear look at the creature. It was not a wild boar at all, but a Giant Panda!

The family began to lose their nerve. Who would dare to kill one of China's national treasures? They would surely be made to pay, perhaps even with their lives. Yet had they bought all that food in vain? Would they forgo the New Year altogether? His wife was complaining, the children were crying, and Wang felt torn. After thinking long and hard, he decided to head to the Fengtong Valley Nature Reserve to seek compensation.

Wang had gone to the right place. He was told that the Nature Reserve would pay for the Spring Festival goods. They also told him that they would provide him with some extra money to buy food to place there for the panda, for only a starving panda could have taken his family's food. The panda should not be treated as a thief, but rather as a guest.

After being given money and food, Mr Wang returned to his home, where the family were happy to hear the resolution of the matter. Now that they had food to spare, they were more than happy to share. They would also let the Giant Panda come and go as he wished, for he was now their distinguished guest.

That evening, the Wang family were very busy, boiling sweet rice and cooking delicious pig bones, all the time with the front door wide open. They once again hid inside the hut, waiting to see whether last night's guest would find the food to his liking.

In the middle of the night, the Giant Panda returned. To their delight, he wolfed down the rice, before chewing noisily on the bones. He climbed on the top of the kitchen range, turning around in satisfaction as if to thank them for the meal. After getting down the

The establishment of the Giant Panda Pedigree database

A database of Giant Pandas Pedigree was established in 1976, and maintained by software from the International Species Information System (ISIS). After many years of revisions and updates, by the end of 2005, information for some 620 animals had been collected. Number one in the database is Sulin, who was caught way back on November 9th 1936. There are currently 188 individuals in captivity, spread across 34 centers and 7 countries worldwide.

panda took a few bones with him to stave off hunger.

The family were as happy as could be, running after the creature with shouts of "come again soon! Do not be a stranger!"

From then on, the panda became a frequent visitor to the Wang home, sometimes for a week or more, others for just a few days. Sometimes he would also bring friends, ranging from just one or two to as many as five. They would saunter in, taking what they wanted, both unfussy and unaffected.

The Wangs were by this stage well accustomed to these visits, and would prepare extra food each winter, which they would place on the top of the kitchen range. At night, they would keep their doors open, allowing the bear to come and go as they pleased, eating what they wanted without the need for pleasantries, as if they were their own children.

Wang also gave the panda the name Lele (literally "happy"). And how could he not be happy? Not only did he have the freedom to roam the great mountain wilderness, but could also visit the Wang home where food was laid on for him. Mr Wang, too, was happy, for if his food budget was tight, the Nature Reserve management would provide him with more. And preparing more food or drink was no effort, for the arrival of Lele brought him great delight.

In the blink of an eye ten years had passed, and Lele was

still very much part of the family. In total he had eaten 100 kilos of grain, 400 kilos of bones and 10 kilos of sugar.

Tuantuan and Yuanyuan

Tuantuan and Yuanyuan were a pair of Giant Pandas given by Mainland China as a gift to the Taiwanese people. The Wolong Center undertook an extensive selection process to this end. First, the pair could not be close relatives; second, they had to be young; third, they had to be well suited in terms of personality and age; fourth, they had to be healthy, active and attractive; fifth, they had to be well-tempered, without

Tuantuan and Yuanyuan at the Wolong Center in 2006

Li Guo (left), and Xu Yalin, charged with looking after Tuantuan and Yuanyuan

bad habits, for example sticking out their tongue or licking their fingers. There were 32 pandas in the selection process, eliminated one by one, until just Tuantuan and Yuanyuan remained. Though the female Yuanyuan was two days older than Tuantuan, the couple were truly a match made in heaven.

After being selected, Tuantuan and Yuanyuan immediately became the focus of the Wolong Center. Experts at the center enlisted the help of experienced keepers Li Guo and Xu Yalin, who were charged with looking after the pandas' eating, drinking and living arrangements, ensuring the animals were kept healthy and happy before their departure. Tuantuan and Yuanyuan for their part did not disappoint, for they grew into strong and healthy specimens. At the time of their selection in January 2006 they weighed a mere 50 kilos, yet by October of the same year they tipped the scales at 80 kilos.

As time passed, young love began to bloom for the two anointed pandas. Yet their carefree days together would soon be dealt a devastating blow.

On May 12th 2008, a huge earthquake measuring 8 on the Richter scale devastated Wenchuan in Sichuan Province, cutting off the Wolong Center, which was situated not far from the epicenter, from the outside world.

Eventually it was discovered that dozens of Giant Pandas had been brought to the safety at the earliest possible moment, and though Tuantuan was among those rescued, Yuanyuan remained missing. A team had already been dispatched to look for her.

News trickled in that three days after going missing, Yuanyuan had eventually been found, and she was immediately returned to Tuantuan's side. What hardship must poor Yuanyuan have endured during this time? What

The lifespan of Giant Pandas

After confirmation from extensive records of Giant Panda bone and teeth samples in the wild, it has been established that Giant Pandas in the wilderness can live up to twenty six years, with most deaths occurring between the ages of twelve and fourteen. In the case of pandas in captivity, the improved nutrition and medical care gives them a considerably longer lifespan, the oldest to date reaching an age of thirty eight.

Giant Pandas and "water inebriation"

Giant Pandas love water, and pandas in the wild are especially fond of drinking flowing stream or source water. If it is frozen over, they will use their front paws to break the ice, and if the water is too shallow they will dig a small hole. Pandas typically drink water once a day, yet they must ensure to drink enough. This often leads to drinking an excessive amount, which makes moving very difficult, sometimes causing them to fall to the ground. For this reason, the locals often refer to it as "Panda water inebriation." A large amount of water allows Giant Pandas to better dissolve their food, aiding their digestion of bamboo.

kind of suffering? These are questions which will forever go unanswered.

After living through such an ordeal, the pair were finally ready to head to Taiwan. Though the young lovers were as happy a couple as one could wish to see, we must also remember that they hail from very different walks of life.

Tuantuan's mother Huamei was a beautiful American-born panda who returned to her native China. His grandmother was Baiyun, and his great-grandfather, i.e. Baiyun's father, was the famed Panpan. Panpan's ancestry was yet more prestigious, covering virtually the half of the captive Giant Panda population. It is easy to see how Tuantuan, a panda from such a proud lineage, would grow up to become the distinguished specimen he is today.

By contrast, Yuanyuan is something of a Cinderella. Her mother Leilei was rescued from the wild, and was found to be missing her front paw. The adorable Leilei was affectionately known as "missing paw mother" by her keepers. Nonetheless, Yuanyuan did not want for anything, for her "missing paw mother" doted on her day and night, giving her protection and attention from the day she was born. Whether it was eating or going to the toilet, Leilei followed her beloved daughter around like a shadow.

And so it was that this proud son of a distinguised family and a coddled girl of humble beginnings were fated to be together. Alike in personality, and strengthened by tragedy, the two became a couple. Today, Tuantuan and Yuanyuan live a rich and satisfied life together, and it only remains for them to continue the love story with a cub of their own.

Chapter Seven

Finally a Place We Can Call Home

Baiyun: Millions of years ago, our earliest ancestors had a territory of their own, their own sanctuary leaving them to live in peace. They could not have dreamed that their descendants would be made to live in captivity, stripped of their freedom and their home. It is not just limited to us, for our compatriots in the wild have also borne the brunt of man's expansion, retreating from the plains to the low mountains, from low mountains to higher mountains, until there is nowhere left to go. Even then they were still driven out by the emergence of new roads and new towns. This continued up until the year the bamboo flowered once again...

Flowering bamboo

For millions of years, bamboo has been periodically going into flower, a process which is necessary for their reproduction. At the same time, Giant Pandas have been growing and expanding as a species. Due to their expansive territory, there were always new places to roam if food became scarce in any one area. However, in 1983, when the bamboo in Qionglai and Minshan Mountains started to flower in large numbers, the pandas had nowhere they could turn. Scientists had long since been awake to the dangers, recognizing that the protection and expansion of Giant Panda natural habitats was essential for them as a species.

Tangjiahe Giant Panda Nature Reserve

The Wanglang Giant Panda Nature Reserve

From 1985 until 1989, the Chinese government once more teamed up with the WWF, and after three years of surveys and two years of planning, the Plans for the Conservation of the Giant Panda and its Habitat, were put into action, which sought not only to strengthen the thirteen existing Giant Panda nature reserves, but also to build a further fourteen centers, as well as restore and repair seventeen zones previously used by Giant Pandas. This would later become the Giant Panda Conservation Project. An investment of 30 million *yuan* was pledged each year, for a total investment of 300 million *yuan*.

In 1993, the World Bank's Global Environment Facility (GEF) set up a council in Beijing, which pledged one million US dollars in order to help eleven of China's nature reserves, and a further five million dollars for restructuring Qinling's Changqing Forest Authority's Changqing Giant Panda Nature Reserve.

The restructuring was designed to encourage the people of Changqing to plant

Flowering bamboo and its effect on Giant Panda survival

A number of species of bamboo can be found in the wild, some of which flower every few decades, while others flower once every century or more. When not flowering, the trees will reproduce by germinating new buds. The flowering process causes all plants of the same type to die off, leading to food shortages for Giant Pandas. In a larger habitat, Giant Pandas are able to find different varieties of bamboo elsewhere. However, in areas where space is limited, the pandas have no place to go, and must instead await their doom.

Shuzheng Falls in the Jiuzhaigou Giant Panda Nature Reserve

The Sanguanmiao station in the Foping Giant Panda Nature Reserve

trees instead of cutting them down. Logging is a lucrative business, while planting trees is costly, and logging needs a large workforce, in comparison to the small number needed for planting. All this meant that the vast majority of people would need to be relocated. The restructuring would force many people off their land, a huge sacrifice on their part.

In spite of the many difficulties, the Changqing Forest Authority's restructuring program had been finalized, and was pressing ahead. It was only after the restructuring that Qinling's Zhouzhi, Foping and Taibai Giant Panda reserves were able to become one large nature reserve, and

Wolong Giant Panda Nature Reserve's Bifeng Gorge Base

Fengtong Valley Nature Reserve's Dashui Valley station

The Wanglang Giant Panda Nature Reserve

Huanglong Giant Panda Nature Reserve

Labahe Giant Panda Nature Reserve

Tangjiahe Giant Panda Nature Reserve

Changqing Giant Panda Nature Reserve's Cang'erya sentry post

only a large nature reserve can provide Giant Pandas with the freedom and food they need, protecting against the decline of the species brought on by inbreeding and dwindling numbers.

From 1950 until 1985, there were 27 state-owned, large-scale forestry companies located in Sichuan and Shaanxi, the two provinces which Giant Pandas call home. These companies were responsible for the destruction of 426,000 hectares of natural forests, causing great upheaval and posing a huge threat to the Giant Pandas in these regions, and turning much of the Giant Pandas' habitat into barren, sparse patches with no chance of regrowth. From 1985 until 1998, China's economy underwent a period of rapid development, and with it the demand for wood also reached a new high. Partial records indicate that in the 35 counties in Sichuan which are home to Giant Pandas, 20 million cubic meters of wood were cut down from 1995 to 1998. From this figure, it can be estimated that

The third Chinese Giant Panda survey in Qinling

the total number in this period would have exceeded 70 million cubic meters.

From 1998, the Chinese government started to implement schemes to protect natural forests, and from September 1998 until April 2000 alone, 40,000 forestry workers were laid off, 8.94 million hectares of natural forest were given protected status, and 28 forestry and logging logistics companies were closed down. At the same time, Shaanxi and Gansu Provinces turned a number of forests previously owned by state-run companies to Giant Panda protected areas, thereby creating large stretches of Giant Panda nature reserve spread across three provinces, providing an excellent habitat for the survival and development of Giant Pandas in the wild.

According to data from the third national Giant Panda survey made in 2003, Giant Pandas were spread across 40 protected areas, covering a total area of 2,175,780 hectares. Up until 2005, the number of Giant Panda protected areas had risen to 56, with an area of 2,900,400 hectares. Of these, 37 were located in Sichuan, covering some 2,099,300 hectares; 14 were in Shaanxi, in an area measuring 311,476 hectares; 5 were in Gansu, covering 489,634 hectares. In terms of geographical distribution, 22 nature reserves are located in the Minshan mountain system, including Jiuzhaigou, Huanglong, Wanglang, Baishuijiang, Tangjiahe, Xuebaoding, and Xiaozhaizi Valley; 11 nature reserves can be found among the Qionglai Mountains, including Fengtong Valley, Wolong, Baishuihe, Longxi, Labahe and Caopo; there are 13 in the Qinling mountain system including Foping, Taibaishan, Changqing, Laoxiancheng, and Motianling; the Liangshan Mountains are home to 6 nature reserves including Mabian Dafengding, Meigu Dafengding, and Heizhugou; Xiaoxiangling contains 3 nature reserves including Gongga Mounatain and Liziping, while Daxiangling contains just one nature reserve, Wawushan.

Chapter Eight

Xiangxiang, the Pioneer of Re-introduction into the Wild

Baiyun: In the last two decades, my brothers and sisters and I in captivity have received the care and attention of humans. Every day we are given specially-prepared meals and fresh bamboo, and have people to clean out our litter for us. When we are fully-grown, experts select mates for us, when we are sick, there are doctors on hand to give us treatment, and when we are giving birth, there are experts to deliver our babies. However, at the bottom of our hearts, we still have one burning desire: returning to the wild, to the place of our ancestors, a place with no walls and no fences, where we can search for food, seek out a mate, and play in complete freedom. A place where we can even fight and scuffle to our hearts' content, until we're bloodied and bruised. That's why I envy young Xiangxiang, who will make the journey back to the wilderness.

The Bifeng Gorge Base team, who made sure the Giant Panda house was clean and stocked with fresh bamboo and cornbread

When the problems of going into heat, impregnation and rearing young were finally solved, the question of releasing pandas in captivity back into the wild was put on the agenda. Between 1997 and 2000, two international conferences were held at the Wolong Center, with the topic of "the possibility of reintroducing Giant Pandas into the wild." Some said that the protection of Giant Pandas' natural habitat was first needed, for without this Giant Pandas would have no territory of their own, and their survival would be impossible. Some felt that after the mass flowering of bamboo in 1983 bamboo in the wild still needed time to recover, and that they should wait till at least 2002 before reintroduction. There were some who said there was a danger of Giant Pandas in captivity exposing pandas in the wild to new diseases. Others believed that the largest problem was that pandas raised in captivity would be unable to fend for themselves in the wild, liable to starve and vulnerable to attack.

Though opinions varied, the one inescapable fact was that the preparation to reintroduce Giant Pandas to the wild was slowly getting underway. In 2003, the Chinese government invested nearly 10 million *yuan* to establish the "China Panda Park" where Giant Pandas could live semi-independently. That same year, Xiangxiang, the first panda to be reintroduced, was selected.

In January 2001, Xiangxiang was born at the Wolong Center. His mother was the center's most beautiful female "No.20," and his grandfather was the famous Panpan.

Xiangxiang was a happy, beautiful, bright cub from a prestigious family, and he could not have been luckier. The first period of reintroduction was in an area of ancient forests which covered 20,000 meters. There he had a vast area to play in, dense jungles, lush bamboo, as well as two servings of cornbread per day. His life there was an extremely free and happy one.

Number 20 with her twins Xiangxiang and Fufu in 2001 (taken by Zhang Guiquan)

However, day by day, he was fed less and less, and could no longer rely on humans to keep him full, nor could he follow them to ask for more. This made the panda upset, and he would often roar or try to bite people when he saw them. This all proved futile, and when hunger got the better of him Xiangxiang was forced to look for food on his own.

Food in the mountains was available all year round, for there are bamboo leaves in the summer, bambo shoots in the autumn, and in winter when food became more scarce the team would provide extra in the form of corn-bread. When Xiangxiang was not quite full, he would ask for more by performing for the team. "Am I not beautiful?" he seemed to say as he climbed up the slopes and slid down. "Am I not funny?" he seemed to say as he took a few steps back up the slope before sliding and rolling back down. "Am I not cute?" he would think as he went up and down again and again before slumping down to the ground and breathing hard. "What about a little reward?" he seemed to beg. Yet all this was to no avail, for his food was still being reduced all the time, and he would still need to find food of his own in order to be satisfied. Xiangxiang was starting to understand that in order to be free he had to rely on himself, and in order to expand his horizons he could not just keep his mouth open and expect to be fed.

Xiangxiang braved Spring, Summer, Autumn and Winter, and the panda who was previously skinny and hungry had now become taller, fatter, and able to feed himself. In

Why reintroduction is necessary

In 2000, the third Chinese Giant Panda Survey was completed, and its results showed that the number of Giant Pandas in the wild stood at roughly 1,600 individuals spread across six mountain systems, namely Qinling, Minshan, Qionglai, Daxiangling, Xiaoxianglin and Liangshan. These six regions had already become completely cut off from one another, and certain Giant Panda habitats within these regions had also become isolated, with panda populations within these small zones falling well below fifty individuals. For these small populations, even without external environmental pressures, the possibility of extinction is still a distinct possibility. Protection of the natural habitat and hunting control are not enough to guarantee the long-term survival of the species. Instead, we must find suitable ways of bringing pandas in captivity back into the wild, thereby bolstering these small populations.

Autumn 2004, Xiangxiang entered the second stage of reintroduction. He was sent to a 200,000 meters area of forests. His territory was vaster, the mountains higher, the forests denser and the lifestyle more independent than before. The hardy young panda was in luck!

Yet there was hardship in store for Xiangxiang. Sleeping on the damp ground, the panda was constantly bitten by lice and leeches, learning the hard way that wet ground was no place to sleep. Facing harsh winds and pouring rain, Xiangxiang did not know where to turn. He would seek out grasslands, dive into bamboo forests, and stick close to trees, yet whatever he tried he could not stop from being drenched. Xiangxiang had no mother to teach him, and he could only find out by trial and error. After diving into tree cavities and niches in cliffs he finally chanced upon a way to keep dry. Xiangxiang made sure not to forget such lessons.

As Spring came around once more, the team had virtually stopped coming, and Xiangxiang could expect not even a crumb of cornbread. But Xiangxiang was not overly concerned. He was already able to find shelter and food for himself, and did not need to be doted on by humans.

One day the team went to secretly watch Xiangxiang, and upon discovering them he let out an almighty roar, flashing his

Xiangxiang after being released back into the wild in 2006 (taken by Zhang Guiquan)

teeth and showing his claws, as if to say "This forest is mine. Get out!"

Xiangxiang was now all grown up and independent, and 200,000 meters were no longer enough. In Spring 2006, the reintroduction program entered its third stage, as the team brought Xiangxiang to the boundless mountains around Wuyi Shed, with nothing but an electronic collar with which to monitor the animal. They were confident that as the next Spring rolled around, Xiangxiang would have found a mate in the wild to cap off a successful reintroduction.

The possibility of reintroduction into the wild

Reintroduction of a species touches upon a number of areas. In 1997, experts convened at the Wolong Center to discuss the feasibility of reintroducing Giant Pandas into the wild, at which many of the experts felt that the time was not yet ripe for reintroduction. In the proceeding six years, China implemented a project designed to protect all natural forests in China, as well as legislation changing farmland back into forests, which resulted in the effective renewal of Giant Panda habitats. At the same time, the numbers of Giant Pandas in captivity were also on the rise, solving not only problems of population maintenance, but also providing an endless source of individuals fit for reintroduction. In 2003, Xiangxiang became the first Giant Panda in captivity to be reintroduced into the wild. Although the plan was ultimately unsuccessful, it provided people with a great deal of experience and a number of important lessons, ensuring that continued efforts in the reintroduction of Giant Pandas are better prepared and more successful.

However, in the Winter of 2006, Xiangxiang was injured and had to be nursed back to health. His two hind legs, both ears, and the left side of his chest had all been badly bitten, as had all his fingers and toes, and he had suffered a broken rib. After his recovery, Xiangxiang was released into the wild once more in Spring 2007. Tragically, Xiangxiang was killed soon afterwards following another attack.

Xiangxiang's death raised a serious debate among experts:

According to the head of the Wolong Center, Zhang Hemin, fighting over territory is quite normal behavior for Giant Pandas, and the willingness of captively-reared pandas to fight those in the wild proves they have not lost their natural fighting instincts.

Professor Pan Wenshi from Beijing University believes that Giant Panda society is a male-dominated society, and that "putting a young, hot-headed panda into the territory of a local bully is akin to signing his death warrant".

According to Fan Zhiyong, Species Program Director for WWF in Beijing, Wuyi Shed has been a key zone of the Giant Panda territory for a long time, and since the Giant Panda population in the region has reached its capacity, there is now no space for the introduction of new individuals.

Giant Panda expert Hu Jinchu believes that artificial rearing should not be taken to excess, and that instead of focusing on population in terms of quantity, attention should be shifted towards quality. By putting more energy into wild individuals and their natural habitat, it becomes easier to maintain the strength and survival chances of the group as a whole.

In conclusion, the reintroduction of Giant Pandas in captivity back to the wild is still very much underway, albeit in a far more cautious and meticulous fashion than before. It is hoped that in the not-too-distant future, Giant Pandas will be able to live like their ancestors in the wild, free to thrive and prosper in a territory they can call their own.